RESPECT*fully*

A Children's Guide to the Halachos of Honoring Parents

Compiled and edited by
Rabbi Ze'ev Greenwald

Illustrated by
Dovid Goldschmidt (GOLD)

FELDHEIM PUBLISHERS
JERUSALEM NEW YORK

Originally published 2003 in Hebrew as
Ani Mechabed Horim

ISBN 1-58330-625-0

Copyright © 2003 by
Rabbi Ze'ev Greenwald
POB 43015 Jerusalem
Tel: 02-652-7417

All rights reserved.
No part of this publication may be translated, reproduced, stored
in a retrieval system or transmitted, in any form or by any means,
electronic, mechanical, photocopying, recording or otherwise,
without prior permission in writing from the publishers.

FELDHEIM PUBLISHERS
POB 35002 / Jerusalem, Israel

202 Airport Executive Park
Nanuet, NY 10954

www.feldheim.com

10 9 8 7 6 5 4 3 2 1

Printed in Israel

Table of Contents

Standing for a Parent.......................5
Keeping the Mitzvah for Yourself 6
Help from Heaven 7
Rabbi Tarfon Honors His Mother 8
The Butcher's Mitzvah......................9
Dama ben Nesina Honors
  His Father.....................................10
Dama ben Nesina's Reward............. 11
How Much Should One Honor
  His Parents..................................12
A Long Life 13
It's Important How You Do It 14
A Son Asked His Father to Work
  and Was Rewarded......................15
The Importance of Studying
  the Laws......................................16
A Child Should Respect His Father
  and Fear His Mother....................17
How Does One Respect Parents? 18
More Ways to Respect Parents 19
Meeting All of Their Needs...............20
Staying in Touch................................21
Standing for Parents 22
"Do It for My Father" 23
Honoring Parents in
  One's Thoughts............................24
Honoring Parents with One's
  Speech, Actions, or Money 25

Give from the Best 26
Be Willing and Cheerful 27
Serve Your Parents Yourself 28
Love for One's Parents......................29
Study Torah and Do Mitzvos 30
Listening Is Part of Honoring 31
The Shabbos Night Blessing.............32
The Yom Kippur Night Blessing........33
Asking for Forgiveness 34
Choosing a Yeshivah........................35
When a Child Doesn't Have
  to Listen..36
Honoring Relatives 37
Honoring Parents After Death 38
Parents Are Rewarded for the Good
  Deeds of Their Children 39
Being in Awe of One's Parents 40
Don't Sit or Stand in Your
  Father's Place 41
Don't Contradict Your Parents..........42
Calling a Parent by His Name...........43
Correcting Parents 44
Waking Parents.................................45
Cursing or Hitting a Parent 46
Medical Treatments 47
Watching What We Say and Think ...48

LETTER OF APPROVAL

Harav Chaim Pinchas Sheinberg
Rosh Yeshiva "Torah Ohr"
Rabbinical Authority of Kiryat Mattersdorf

I was pleased to receive the special book on honoring parents, written by Harav Hagaon Rav Ze'ev Greenwald. The subjects are written about in pleasant and lucid language, clearly set out, in good taste and with attention to detail, and he appears to have produced an accurate work.

Although I make a practice not to give endorsements, especially concerning a book on Halacha, nevertheless, because the contents are appropriate and important, I bless him that the wellspring of his knowledge should overflow and his words be accepted in the Torah world.

With Torah blessings,
Chaim Pinchas Sheinberg

PREFACE

It says in *Kiddushin* 30-31:

Our Sages learn that there are three partners within a man: *Hakadosh Baruch Hu*, and his father and mother. When a man honors his parents, G-d says: "I consider it as if I was living among them and he had honored Me."

Chazal stress the importance of this mitzvah and its vast influence. We therefore felt the necessity to publish a book from which every child could learn the laws pertaining to this mitzvah and appreciate its great value.

In our book we attempt to teach the laws of honoring parents in an interesting, eye-catching and captivating manner. The reader, i.e. the child, will relate to the pictures and the situations they depict, and gradually absorb the important laws. Reading this book will also inspire the child to practice these laws.

Educators were consulted throughout the planning of this book, and their recommendations were our guiding light. We offer our heartfelt thanks to all those who assisted us with their guidance, advice and direction. We also appreciate the help we merited from Above while editing this book and pray that our work will benefit the reader.

Standing for a Parent

Click clack, click clack. The sound of footsteps echoed around the room. When Rabbi Yosef heard this sound, he knew that his mother was approaching. He quickly stood up to honor her, and said, "I will rise in honor of the Shechinah, which has just entered." (*Kiddushin* 31b)

Keep the Mitzvah for Yourself

Hearing his father coming, Avimi always ran to open the door. Although Avimi had five sons, he would not let any of them do it. Avimi wanted this mitzvah for himself. (*Kiddushin* 31a) About this, Rabbi Abahu said, "My son Avimi has truly fulfilled the mitzvah of honoring me."

Help from Heaven

Rabbi Abahu asked his son, Avimi, to bring him a glass of water. Avimi went to get it and, while he was away, his father nodded off to sleep. Avimi returned with the water and found his father asleep. Avimi stood quietly before his father waiting for his father to awaken.

There was a Midrash on a chapter in *Tehillim* that Avimi had never fully understood, but standing there, waiting for his father, it became clear. In the merit of the mitzvah of honoring one's parent, Avimi received Hashem's help in understanding a difficult Torah passage. From here we learn that one should make a special effort in the mitzvah of honoring his parents. (*Kiddushin* 31a)

Rabbi Tarfon Honors His Mother

Rabbi Tarfon had an elderly mother who found it difficult to climb onto her bed. Rabbi Tarfon would show her respect by getting on his hands and knees beside her bed and letting her use him as a step every morning and every evening.

One day, while discussing the mitzvah of honoring parents with the other Sages in the *Beis HaMidrash*, Rabbi Tarfon told the Sages about his unusual manner of helping his mother. They responded, "You still have not fulfilled half of the mitzvah of honoring parents! If your mother took a wallet, with all your money inside it, and threw it into the sea, can you guarantee that you would not be upset with her?"
(*Kiddushin* 32b)

The Butcher's Mitzvah

Rabbi Yehoshua ben Ilem was a *tzaddik*, who spent his days learning Torah and doing good deeds. One night, asleep in bed, Rabbi Yehoshua had a dream. In the dream he was told, "Be happy Yehoshua. For you and Nanus the butcher will sit together and have the same portion in *Gan Eden*." Rabbi Yehoshua woke up and was very puzzled by this strange dream. He thought to himself, "Ever since I was born, I have been very careful to work hard at my Torah study and to fear Hashem. I never went anywhere without wearing my *tallis* and *tefillin*. I have had eighty students learning Torah from me! And now I find out that my reward is no greater than that of an ordinary butcher!" Rabbi Yehoshua told his students that until he found out about Nanus the butcher, he would not enter the *Beis HaMidrash*. Who was this man who would be his partner in *Gan Eden*? From town to town, city to city, they searched, asking everyone they met if they knew Nanus the butcher. Finally, they came to a city and asked, "Do you know of Nanus the butcher?"

"Why are you interested in an ordinary butcher?" was the reply. Rabbi Yehoshua asked, "What sort of things does he do?" "If you are so interested in him, why don't you see for yourself?" the townspeople answered. Nanus was soon told that Rabbi Yehoshua was looking for him. "What can the great Sage Rabbi Yehoshua possibly want with me?" he thought to himself. The people of the town wanted to take him to the great Rabbi, but Nanus thought that they were playing a trick on him and he wouldn't go. So, Rabbi Yehoshua himself went to look for Nanus the butcher.

When Nanus saw Rabbi Yehoshua approaching him, he fell to his knees and asked, "Why has the Crown of Israel come to his servant?" Rabbi Yehoshua answered, "I wanted to speak with you. Tell me Nanus, what do you do?"

Nanus replied, "My master, I am a butcher, and I have elderly parents who are unable to take care of themselves. Every day I dress, feed, and wash them myself." Immediately, Rabbi Yehoshua stood up and kissed him on the head. He said, "My son, fortunate are you that you are so involved in serving your parents, and fortunate am I to have you as a partner in *Gan Eden*." From this story, we see how great is the reward for honoring parents. Even simple people can receive a portion in *Gan Eden* that equals that of the great Rabbis by fulfilling this mitzvah. (*Sefer HaDoros*, Part 3)

Dama ben Nesina Honors His Father

Our Sages tell many stories about how Dama ben Nesina, a non-Jew from Ashkelon, honored his parents. According to Rabbi Eliezer, the Sages offered him six hundred thousand gold dinars if he would sell them a certain precious stone right away for the *Kohen Gadol*'s special breastplate. But Dama ben Nesina turned down their offer because the key to the chest of jewels was under his sleeping father's pillow, and he did not want to disturb him. (*Kiddushin* 31a)

Dama ben Nesina's Reward

Hashem rewarded Dama ben Nesina for not disturbing his father when he was sleeping, by having a red heifer (*parah adumah*) born to his herd. The Sages came to buy it to use in the process they followed to make people *tahor* and they were willing to pay any price to get it. Dama ben Nesina told them, "All I want is the money I lost because I would not take the key from under my father's pillow the last time you came and wanted to buy a precious stone." Rabbi Chanina said, "If Hashem rewards this man, who is not commanded to honor his parents and yet does so, how much more will He reward someone who is commanded to honor his parents and does so." (*Kiddushin* 31a)

How Much Should One Honor His Parents?

The Sages used Dama ben Nesina as an example of how it is better for a man to control himself rather than to lessen his parent's honor. The Sages once asked Rabbi Elazar how much we must honor our parents. Rabbi Elazar said, "You're asking me? Go and ask Dama ben Nesina!"

Dama ben Nesina was a mayor and an army commander. Once he was standing in front of his soldiers when his mother came up to him and slapped him so hard that her sandal fell off her foot. In response, Dama calmly bent down, picked up the sandal, and handed it back to his mother so that she would not feel uncomfortable. (*Peah* 1:1) Rav Dimi said, "Dama ben Nesina was once sitting with important Roman noblemen. He was all dressed up, wearing a beautiful silk cloak embroidered with gold thread. Along came Dama's mother, who ripped off his cloak, hit him on the head, and spat in his face. Dama ben Nesina did nothing back to embarrass her."(*Kiddushin* 31a)

A Long Life

Honoring parents is one of the few mitzvos where the Torah clearly tells us what reward we will receive for it: we will merit a long life.

Rabbi Abba bar Kahana says (*Yerushalmi Peah* 1:1), "The Torah compares one of the easiest mitzvos to one of the hardest. One of the easiest mitzvos to perform is that of sending a mother bird away from her nest before taking her chicks. One of the hardest mitzvos is honoring parents. About both of them it is written (*Shemos* 20:12 and *Devarim* 24:7), 'so that you will live long.' "

It's Important How You Do It

We are taught that it is not so much what we do for our parents as how we do it. If we give our parents a really nice meal, but stare angrily at them while they eat it, we have not shown them respect and we will be punished for it (*Shulchan Aruch, Yoreh De'ah* 240:4).

A Son Asked His Father to Work and Was Rewarded

The Talmud (*Yerushalmi Pe'ah* 1:1) tells us about a man who earned a living grinding wheat. This man had an elderly father whom he looked after and cared for. One day, the evil king sent a message to every family that worked grinding wheat to send one person from their family to come and work for him.

The king would make his workers work very hard and would sometimes beat those workers harshly, and shame and embarrass them. So, the caring son gently said to his father, "You grind the wheat instead of me, and I will work for the king instead of you." In this case, Hashem rewarded the son for sending his father to work.

The Importance of Studying the Laws

Every day, we get many chances to honor our parents, but we don't know exactly how to do it. For this reason, it is important that we study all the laws about how to honor our parents and know them well. (*Yesod V'Shoresh HaAvodah, Sha'ar HaNitzutz,* Chapter 2)

We should also study the stories in the Torah and what our Sages say about how to treat our parents. (*Sefer Meah Shearim, Sha'ar* 16)

A Child Should Respect His Father and Fear His Mother

When the Torah commands us to respect our parents, the father is mentioned before the mother in the verse, "Respect your father and your mother" (*Shemos* 20:12, *Devarim* 5:15). However, when we are told to fear out parents, the Torah mentions the mother first in the verse, "Each person should treat his mother and father with fear" (*Vayikra* 19:3). Why does it do this?

Rebbi said (*Kiddushin* 30-31), "Hashem, the Creator of the Universe, knows that a child naturally wants to honor his mother more than his father, because his mother is more gentle with him. For this reason, it mentions honoring the father before honoring the mother. And it is known that a child normally fears his father more than his mother, because he teaches him Torah, so the Torah mentions fearing the mother first."

How Does One Respect Parents?

How should we show respect for our parents? The Talmud (*Kiddushin* 31b) answers that we should give them to eat and drink. This applies especially when it is hard for them to take care of themselves. This means for example when they are old or sick or weak, or even when they are tired and need help.

More Ways to Respect Parents

We should also dress and cover them (if they need our help) and walk with them when they come into the house or leave. (*Kiddushin* 31b)

Meeting All of Their Needs

We have already discussed ways in which a person can honor his parents. But there are many other ways. For example, he can: Shop for them, make sure their home is comfortable and neat, and if they are not feeling well, make sure that they have the doctors and medicines they need. He can also help by lifting heavy packages for them or doing other things that they find difficult.

Each of us should think of ways that we can honor and help our parents.

Staying in Touch

If you aren't living at home (and this includes sleeping away at yeshiva or camp, as well as growing up and getting married), it is a mitzvah to phone or write your parents regularly so that they will not worry about how you are.

A grown-up child who doesn't live at home should visit his parents regularly. He should also invite his parents over to visit him, welcoming them warmly when they come and showing them respect. For instance, a son should let his parents wash their hands first for a meal and should serve them their food first.

Standing for Parents

Just as we must stand in honor of our Rabbis and teachers, we must also stand for our parents (*Rambam, Hilchos Mamrim* 6:3; see also *Shulchan Aruch* #240:7). The following are some of the laws about standing:

Both sons and daughters must stand to honor their parents (*Chayei Adam* 67:7). You must stand as soon as you see your parents in the distance and keep standing until you no longer see them or until you meet them.

You do not have to stand for your parents if they are not in the same room or place as you. This is because it would not be clear that you were standing in order to honor them.

You only have to stand up for your parents twice a day - once in the morning and once in the evening. If there are people in the room who do not know that you already stood up for your parents that day, you should stand up again. According to some, you should stand up whenever you see your parents - even if that means 100 time a day. The Sephardim do this.

"Do It for My Father"

If you need to ask someone for a favor, instead of saying, "Do it for my sake," say "Do it for my father's sake." The reason is that the father receives honor when the son mentions his name respectfully and when people do the son a favor for his sake. (*Kiddushin* 31b)

If a child knows that he can get something either for his father's sake or for his own, he should ask it for his father's sake. (*Yoreh De'ah* 240:6)

Honoring Parents in One's Thoughts

The mitzvah of honoring our parents means to treat them with respect, speak to them with respect, and to think that they are special. If we really don't respect them, but act like we do, we are just putting on a show, as it says in *Yeshayah* 29:13, "They honored me with mouths and lips, but their hearts were far away from me." If we come to think well of our parents, it will help us speak to them and act toward them with respect. Each child should respect his parents in his heart and feel that they are important members of the community, even if other people do not think so (*Chayei Adam, Klal* 67:3). This is the meaning of honoring parents.

Honoring Parents with One's Speech, Actions, or Money

We should speak to our parents in a calm, gentle, and respectful way, as we would to a king or a queen. We should also help them whenever they need it, whether with our actions or with our money. This is the meaning of honoring our parents (*Sefer Charedim* 12:1-2).

Give from the Best

Whenever we do a mitzvah or help another Jew, we should do it using the nicest things that we have (*Yoreh De'ah* 248:8). If we build a synagogue, it should be even more beautiful than our own home. If we feed the hungry, it should be from the finest food. If we give clothes to the needy, they should be from the nicest that we own. We learn this from the Torah, which teaches us, "All the choice fats should be (offered up as a sacrifice) to Hashem" (*Vayikra* 3:16). This is how we should honor our parents. Whatever we give them should be from the best that we have.

Be Willing and Cheerful

We should honor our parents cheerfully and willingly, being careful never to get angry at them. Bad thoughts about our parents can cause us to lose all of our reward for honoring our parents or even bring a punishment.

We should try to think about what our parents might need so that we can bring it to them before they even ask for it.

Serve Your Parents Yourself

A person should always serve his parents himself, instead of letting someone else do it. This is true even if one is already an adult, a Torah scholar, or a very important person.

Also, it says in *Bereishis* 46:29, "Yosef bridled his chariot and went to meet Yisrael, his father, in the land of Goshen." Rashi explains that Yosef did this himself, even though he was a very important man in the government of Mitzrayim, so that he could go out to meet his father more quickly. Ralbag learns from this verse that it is a mitzvah even for a government leader to serve his parents as much as he can.

Love for One's Parents

Feeling love for our parents is a very important part of the mitzvah of honoring one's parents. The Zohar in *Parashas KiTetzei* says, "A person should take care of his parents, love them more than himself and believe that everything he has is less important than doing what his parents ask."

We are taught that we should feel the same love for our parents as we feel for Hashem (which means that we should love them more than any other person).

Study Torah and Do Mitzvos

One of the best ways in which we can honor our parents is to learn Torah and do lots of mitzvos. Not only will this give them a great deal of pleasure, but they will receive a reward from Hashem. Also, people will bless and respect the parents even more when they see that they have raised a good child.

Listening Is Part of Honoring

Part of honoring our parents is listening to them when they tell us that we are doing something wrong. They are only trying to keep us on the path of Torah and mitzvos.

The Shabbos Night Blessing

Does your father give you a special *berachah* after he comes home from shul on Shabbos night? Boys are told, "May Hashem make you like Efraim and Menashe." Girls are told, "May Hashem make you like Sarah, Rivkah, Rachel and Leah."

Afterwards, the verses of the *Kohanim*'s blessing are recited: "May Hashem bless you and watch over you. May He shine His face towards you and be gracious to you. May Hashem lift up His face to you and give you peace" (*Bemidbar* 6:24-26). Because this blessing comes from the depths of the heart, it is likely to be fulfilled (*Sefer Pele Yoetz, Berachos*).

The Yom Kippur Night Blessing

It is a custom for the father to bless his sons and daughters before going to shul on the evening of Yom Kippur (see *Chayei Adam* 144:19 and the Yom Kippur *machzor*). He asks Hashem to give them a good life, where they will fear Hashem and be successful in studying Torah (*Mateh Efraim*, #619 *Alef Hamagen*).

Asking for Forgiveness

On the eve of Yom Kippur, we should ask our parents to forgive us for anything bad we did to them over the past year (*Sefer Ben Ish Chai, Year 1, Vayelech* #6). In fact, anytime we hurt our parents we should immediately say we are sorry and ask for their forgiveness.

Choosing a Yeshivah

A son can go to any yeshivah that he thinks will be better for his Torah study, even if his father opposes it because of safety concerns (*Shulchan Aruch Yorah De'ah* 240:25). However, since choosing a yeshivah is the most important step in a boy's life, he should ask his (parents and) teachers what they think he should do and then think very carefully before deciding. If he decides to study in a different city, he should still stay in touch with his parents because they will want to hear from him.

When a Child Doesn't Have to Listen

If our parents tell us to do something that is against the Torah, we should not listen to them. Since both the commandment to honor our parents and the Torah came from Hashem, we should not listen to our parents when they tell us to do something that goes against His words. If a parent commands his son not to speak to a certain person or not to forgive a certain person for a long time, the son should not obey him (*Shulchan Aruch, Yoreh De'ah* 240:15,16).

Honoring Relatives

In addition to respecting parents, a person must respect other relatives as well (*Shulchan Aruch, Yoreh De'ah* 240:21-24).

If your father married a second time, you must show respect to his wife, even though she is not your mother. Similarly, if your mother remarried, you must show respect to her husband. It is fitting to continue honoring them even after your parent is no longer alive.

You must respect your older brother, even if he is only a half brother.

A person must be respectful towards his parents-in-law. We find that King David treated his father-in-law King Shaul with honor, and called him, "Father" (*Shemuel* I 24:12).

A person must also honor his father's father. However, before he honors his grandfather, he should honor his father.

Honoring Parents After Death

Some people honor their parents while they are alive because they are afraid of them or because they want to inherit their money after they are dead. A child who honors his parent after he has died does it for pure reasons, and it is counted as though he did it while the parent was still alive (*Semachos* 9).

How does a child honor a parent after he has died? During the first twelve months after the parent's death, while saying something in his father's name, he can say, "My father, my teacher, may I be his atonement" (Rashi says that this means that if anything bad is going to happen to the father in the World Above, it should happen to the child instead). After this he should say, "May his memory be a blessing for eternal life."

Parents Are Rewarded for the Good Deeds of Their Children

When children study Torah and do mitzvos, they give pleasure and credit to their parents even after they have died. This is a way of honoring them. We are told that when a son comes up with *chiddushim*, new ways to understand the Torah, this brings honor to his parents' souls - particularly on Shabbos (*Pele Yoetz, Chiddush*). Since parents bring their child into the world, whenever he does good it is because of how they brought him up, and they get rewarded for it.

Being in Awe of One's Parents

Once every seven years, in the times of the holy Temple, the entire Jewish people would gather in Jerusalem for Hakhel. A special portion of the Torah would be read to them. According to one opinion, the portion read was taken from *Vayikra*. It was chosen because it contains many important ideas from the Torah. Rabbi Levi said (*Vayikra Rabbah* 24:5), "This portion was read because it includes the command, 'Each man shall be in awe of his mother and father' (*Vayikra* 19:3)."

The Talmud explains what awe means, and the following pages tell us how we can show it.

אִישׁ אִמּוֹ וְאָבִיו תִּירָאוּ...

Don't Sit or Stand in Your Father's Place

If your father has a specific chair that he sits on at home, or stands in a certain place where he meets his friends, you should not sit or stand there. You also should not sit in your father's chair in shul (*Shulchan Aruch* 240:2). This shows your awe of him and also that you do not consider yourself to be his equal. (*Chayei Adam* 67:8)

Don't Contradict Your Parents

Showing awe means not contradicting what your parents said (*Kiddushin* 31b). A child may not say to someone who disagrees with his parents, "I agree with you" (*Shach* 240:2). If your parent disagrees with someone, you should not even say, "I agree with my parent."

If a child is studying Torah, he is only allowed to disagree with his father if his father isn't there, but this must be done in a respectful way (*ibid, Taz* #3). There is an opinion that he's not allowed to do it even then (*ibid, Shach* #2). About everyday things, a son shouldn't disagree with his father, even if he isn't there. But he is allowed to ask difficult questions and offer answers when they are studying together. A son may even give a halachic ruling. In addition, if a father asks a son for his opinion, he may say it even if it contradicts his father's opinion.

Calling a Parent by His Name

You should never call your parent by his name, or even say his name (*Kiddushin* 31b). It doesn't matter whether the parent is in the same room as you or not. Instead you should call them, "My father, my teacher," or, "My mother, my teacher." Some Rabbis say that you may mention your parent's name if you put a title before it, such as "My father, my teacher," or "Reb." If you are called up to the Torah, and are asked your father's name, you should add a title before it. For example, if your name is Aaron, and your father's name is Moshe, you should say that your name is "Aaron ben Reb Moshe."

What happens if one of your friends has the same name as one of your parents? If your parent's name is uncommon, when you speak to your friend, you should pronounce his name differently. Some Rabbis permit saying your friend's name normally, if your parent is not present.

If your parent's name is a popular one and you have a friend by that name, you can call your friend by his name as long as your parent isn't there. *Chayei Adam* #67 says that today you can say your parent's first name when calling another person, even if your parent is there, because today parents don't mind.

Correcting Parents

If you should see your father (or mother) do something that is not permitted in the Torah, don't call out, "Father, you have done a sin!" This will only upset and embarrass him. Instead, you should say, "Father, it is written in the Torah such-and-such" (Rashi says that it should be said gently, so that your father will understand why you are mentioning this).

The Rambam writes (in *Hilchos Mamrim* 6:11) that the best way to correct a parent is to put it in the form of a question: "Doesn't it say in the Torah such-and-such?" Then, it looks as if you really want to know something, and not as if you are criticizing.

It is so important to respect and honor parents, that even if they do something that is not permitted in the Torah, you must still show them respect and not (G-d forbid) make them feel embarrassed or sad.

Waking Parents

When your parents are sleeping, you must be very careful not to make a lot of noise or to speak loudly, so that you don't wake them, because this would upset them. However, if you are sure your father wouldn't mind being awakened for something, like a business deal, then it is a mitzvah to wake him up since that is what he would want (*Chayei Adam* 67:11). Also you may awaken your father to go and pray in shul, or to do a mitzvah, since everyone must show respect to Hashem (*Sefer Chassidim* #337). But if these mitzvos can be done later, after your father wakes up, then you should not wake him. Of course, if your father asks you to wake him at a certain time so that he can do something, then you should.

Cursing or Hitting a Parent

It is forbidden to curse or hit our parents. The Torah says this is a great sin and gives very severe punishments for doing this. We are not allowed to cause them a bruise or do anything that might make them bleed.

Medical Treatments

If one's parents need a medical procedure that might cause even a small amount of bruising or bleeding, the child should ask a Rav whether he can perform it or whether he should get someone else to do it. When there is no one else to treat the parents and they are in distress, the Rambam permits the child to treat them.

Watching What We Say and Think

We must never think or speak badly of our parents. The Torah (*Devarim* 27:16) tells us, "Cursed is one who belittles his parent, and all the nation said 'Amen'." This is a hard law to keep, because it is difficult not to think badly of our parents from time to time (*Ben Ish Chai*). We must especially guard ourselves from saying bad things about our parents, because it is very easy to let something slip out, even if we really do not think poorly of them.